A Guide to
Belbin Team Roles

*How to increase personal and
team effectiveness*

Max Isaac

Kevin Carson

From 3Circle Partners

3Circle Partners works with businesses that are looking to enhance value by driving better performance and/or maximizing their investments in improvement programs. Our customized approach will accelerate your organization's performance through strong leadership and strategy, solid internal processes for superior execution, and effective interactions.

Acknowledgments

Thanks to Meredith Belbin for his support over the years and allowing us to cite his material. We would also like to thank Sue Reynard and Carole Johnson for their invaluable contributions to this book.

www.3CirclePartners.com

877-333-3606 or 416-483-7380

Published by Bridge Publishing

ISBN 978-0-9862956-7-6

Table of Contents

Appendix 2: Interpreting a Belbin Report

Introduction

Irene, Carlos, Sandy, and Roger have been brought together in a development team charged with designing a new mortgage service for their bank. Irene, as the bank manager, is serving as the team leader and has selected the other members. She picked Carlos because he knows the most about mortgages, Sandy because she is an experienced loan officer, and Roger because he was involved in several service design projects in the past.

Everything goes well for about a month. The team has lively discussions around setting goals and holds very productive meetings with customers to identify critical needs. But then things go awry. Irene, Carlos, and Roger have come up with several potential service designs, but can't seem to finalize the definition. They keep thinking of more and more different options to build into the service. Sandy, on the other hand, sees time slipping by, but doesn't feel like she can stand up to the other team members to enforce deadlines.

If your company is like this bank, the selection of team members is a straightforward process conducted by a manager or executive. Like Irene, your managers or executives choose teams based on common criteria such as subject matter expertise, possession of relevant skills or knowledge, availability, a personal stake in the outcome of the project, and position within the company.

But is that really the best approach? You've probably seen teams like this one that perform very well for a while but then get bogged down—or ones that never seem to get out of the project definition phase. The failure of many teams makes it clear that perhaps we need to consider whether something else is going on; that perhaps we need to consider whether a given collection of individuals will work well together.

In fact, this latter approach does provide insights into what exactly makes a team effective. The study of team composition began in the 1970s when Meredith Belbin, a researcher in the United Kingdom, spent nine years intensively researching the factors that made teams either effective or ineffective. The outcome of this research is his seminal work on Team Role Theory, which explains why it is the mix of different team skills within the team that is the primary determinant of team effectiveness. In research trials, Belbin and his colleagues were able to accurately predict which teams of executives would do well in management simulations and which would falter. The findings have since been applied worldwide to real-life business situations.

For our purposes here, the critical outcome from Belbin's research is that the criteria his research revealed as being crucial to team success bear little to no resemblance to standard team-selection criteria, such as those listed above. More importantly, while the criteria in widespread use have little to no correlation to team success, Belbin's Team Role

Theory has great predictive power. And it shares the virtue of being relatively easy to implement in the real world.

In this section, we will quickly recap Belbin's research. We will then explore its application to you as an individual and to your teams. We'll also explore the experience of Irene's mortgage team in more depth. But first some background.

CHAPTER 1

Belbin's Research: Discovering Team Roles

Belbin's research was a cooperative effort between the Industrial Training Research Unit based in Cambridge and Henley College, the oldest business school in the U.K. Henley's approach to training was to form groups of ten or eleven managers into what they called syndicates.

These syndicates were carefully selected so that there was a balance of backgrounds and experience in the group. The use of syndicates in learning led to a growing interest in management teams. Henley had noticed that some syndicates did better than others. This became the subject of much debate. This is where Meredith Belbin came into the picture. A research initiative was established to undertake a study of what made some teams more successful than others. Over a period of nine years, Belbin and his colleagues at Henley studied participants assigned to small teams which competed against each other in management simulations.

Phase 1: Teams of High Intelligence

An early hypothesis was that the success of these teams would be highly correlated to the individual excellence of team members (that is, the teams with the smartest people would finish highest). As a matter of course, Belbin administered standardized intelligence tests to the students. Then he intentionally put those with the highest scores together in teams (dubbed "Apollo" teams after the American space program's rocket scientists).

It may not surprise you that when the results of the simulations were analyzed, the Apollo teams typically finished close to last or dead last! They were difficult to manage, prone to destructive and unresolved debates, and often more internally competitive than collaborative. In many cases, one individual's actions would intentionally or unintentionally undermine those of another team member.

There were a few successful Apollo teams. Like all Apollo teams, their members were highly intelligent, but the people on the successful Apollo teams tended to be less assertive. The team also had a chairperson (we'd call that person a team leader nowadays) who was able to corral the talents of the team members and also counteract any tendency for members to sit back and be passive. In addition, the successful Apollo teams had explicit conversations about how to compensate for such a uniformly intellectual group. With these factors and strategies in place, they managed to develop and execute effective strategies without devolving into internal squabbling.

Phase 2: Teams of like orientations

The rare successful exceptions to the Apollo pattern became the basis for a shift away from purely intellect-based hypotheses towards ones that incorporated more behavioral elements. As part of his research, Belbin administered personality tests in addition to intelligence tests. He then formed "pure teams" of individuals with like personalities to see if there was any advantage to certain personality profiles.

While there were slight performance differences among the various pure teams, no personality type was found to be universally effective for a homogeneous team. Rather, their personalities tended to make them well-suited to certain types of tasks and ill-suited to others. During the multi-day management simulation, each of the pure teams' weak points were exposed at some point, and overall the teams were deemed to be less-than-optimal performers.

Phase 3: Searching for balance

The focus of Belbin's investigation now turned to achieving balanced teams that could combine the best attributes of the different "pure teams" all of whom excelled at some tasks and struggled with others. Here the challenge was to isolate which attributes significantly contributed to enhanced team performance.

Because the results of the teams were measurable and the composition of team members was known from the standpoint of individual test scores on personality, intelligence, and other tests, the researchers were able to analyze what combinations were present in successful teams and absent in failed teams. As the study progressed, Belbin and his team developed descriptions for nine different **team roles**, skills and contributions that proved useful on teams. Here is a quick recap of what Belbin discovered about team roles:

One of the first critical attributes to emerge in the research was **creativity**, which was fulfilled by two distinct types of contributions:

- The creative contribution to the team came to be called the **Plant** role by Belbin because he intentionally "planted" people with this skill into teams. When these individuals were given the opportunity by the team to be creative, the team's performance consistently improved. When the Plant role was suppressed or overlooked, the team failed to harness the power of their creativity and performance suffered.

- A second category associated with new ideas is the **Resource Investigator** role. The differentiation is that while the Plant role relies on internal thinking to come up with ideas, the people who play the Resource Investigator role well are adept at using other people (often outside the team) to collect new ideas or discover opportunities that the team could incorporate into their strategies and actions.

Whether or not a team is able to capture these ideas seems to hinge on how the team is managed by its leader or chairperson. Again, Belbin found this team need being filled in two very different ways:

- The more successful chairperson had a specific set of attributes that were later embodied in a team role called **Coordinator**. These individuals are seen to be trusting and accepting of others, dominant, and committed to goals, as well as calm in a crisis. These attributes allow them to guide and facilitate the group effectively, as well as to orchestrate the assignment of tasks to the best-suited individuals.

• Another role that emerged during this phase, that of **Monitor Evaluator**, proved to be a vital contributor to team success. People with this capability often are serious-minded and largely immune to infectious enthusiasm. Having the Monitor Evaluator role well-executed enables discovery of hidden flaws in an argument, allowing others to change their minds based on logic and reasoning.

Another key role that emerged was the **Implementer**, people who made sure that things got done. The Implementer role contribution is to be practical, realistic, and structured, ensuring that necessary tasks are performed. It is disciplined, orderly, and skilled at planning. Its presence on a team ensured that decisions would be turned into results.

Another style of leadership that Belbin identified only after his research became more widely known has been dubbed **Shaper**, a role that is in many ways the opposite of the collaborative Coordinator role.

The contribution of the Shaper role is to bring energy to the team, challenge thinking, and stimulate action. Sometimes, this can be seen as argumentative and pushy. The presence of decidedly different working styles in a team inevitably leads to interpersonal conflicts, in some cases so extreme that two individuals are "toxic opposites" and cannot work together. In other cases, some individuals get overlooked or shut out. The antidote to these pitfalls rests in a role called the **Team Worker**, people who can make a timely intervention to restore balance amongst the team members. The Team Worker role's well-developed social and political skills—combined with a willingness to be supportive of others—have a lubricating effect on teams, maintaining morale and rapport within the team.

The final two roles to emerge were related to getting the details right.

- **Completer Finisher**: This role requires a detail-orientation, and has a desire to see things through to the end. It serves to ensure both the completion of tasks and that quality standards are set and met. It also excels at finding errors and omissions.

- **Specialist**: While not a significant factor in the management simulation at Henley, the role of Specialist was of critical significance when Belbin began applying the theory to real-world settings. In real situations, there is often a need for specialized, expert-level knowledge, without which the team would certainly fail.

The descriptions of these nine roles are summarized in Table 1.A (next page). In addition, there is a quick reference guide to all nine roles at the end of this section.

Table 1.A: Summary of Teams Roles

Role	Contribution
Plant (PL)	Creative, imaginative, unorthodox. Solves difficult problems.
Resource Investigator (RI)	Extroverted, enthusiastic, communicative. Explores opportunities. Develops contacts.
Coordinator (CO)	Mature, confident, a good chairperson. Clarifies goals, promotes decision-making, delegates well.
Shaper (SH)	Challenging, dynamic, thrives on pressure. Has the drive and courage to overcome obstacles.
Monitor / Evaluator (ME)	Sober, strategic and discerning. Sees all options. Judges accurately.
Team Worker (TW)	Cooperative, mild, perceptive and diplomatic. Listens, builds, averts friction, calms the waters.
Implementer (IMP)	Disciplined, reliable, conservative and efficient. Turns ideas into practical actions.
Completer / Finisher (CF)	Painstaking, conscientious. Searches out errors and omissions. Delivers on time.
Specialist (SP)	Single-minded, self-starting, dedicated. Provides knowledge and skills in rare supply.

Optimal Team Size

Belbin's research findings do NOT mean that a team must be composed of nine individuals, each playing one role. As noted above, most of us are capable of being effective at more than one role. For the sake of simplicity, let us assume that an individual can play three of the nine roles very well (this capability is not unusual). It could be possible then to have a balanced team with as few as three people.

However, in practice the optimal team size is four to six individuals. With less than four people, a team is likely to have voids, or unfilled team roles. With more than six, the roles are usually all covered, but surpluses become commonplace. (We will cover the problems associated with voids and surpluses in greater detail in Chapter 2.) Furthermore in teams that have more than six members, the sense of team tends to break down. Once a team reaches about ten people, "inner circles" tend to form as team members intuitively gravitate back to a more functional size.

Validation of the Belbin Model

The proof of a theory is its reliability and predictive capability. Belbin's theory that teams composed in a balanced fashion will generally outperform those that are imbalanced was tested in multiple iterations of the management simulation. The results of two series of trials—the first in 1976 and the second in 1979—are shown in the graphs on the next page.

Figure 1.1: Results of Belbin's Research

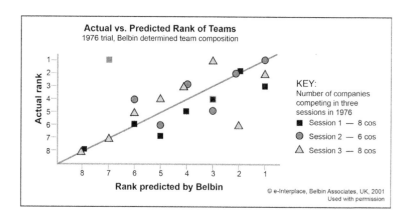

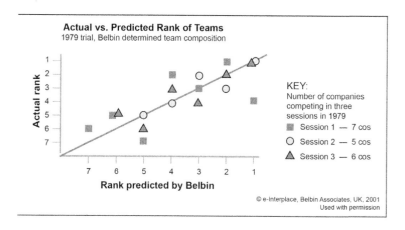

Unbalanced Teams Can Succeed

The comparison between these graphs is interesting because, in 1976, Belbin himself selected the teams based on the results of his research, while in 1979, he made the predictions after the team composition had been set by the

Henley administrators. As you can see, Belbin's predictions were remarkably accurate. There isn't a perfect correlation between the prediction and actual results in either case, but, in most cases teams finished within one or two ranks of the prediction. Furthermore, in the cases of discrepancies, anecdotal evidence gathered in interviews indicated that while the team was balanced "on paper," they were not so in practice, because of the way the team organized itself or because an individual chose to contribute in some way other than their best Team Role.

Belbin's Team Role Theory gives an organization much more predictive power (and thus control) over team effectiveness than is possible with other methods. These results established Belbin as a world leader in behavioral science research.

CHAPTER 2

Applications of Belbin's Insights

Because Belbin's research was focused on teams, our major application of his theory will reside at that level. However, we have found that the ideas that help individuals best contribute to teams also have profound implications for their daily jobs. As a result, we will divide our application discussions into team and individual topics. We'll talk first about how to analyze the team role strengths for individual team members, then how teams and individuals can apply that information.

Individual Team Role Reports

The analysis of where a team is strong or weak starts by having each member do a Team Role report, which is a combination of ratings they give themselves and that others give them on skills and behaviors related to the nine roles. Each person completes a questionnaire that asks about how they deal with different situations; four to six others (called Observers by Belbin) also evaluate that person on what behaviors they see the person displaying in the workplace.

A software algorithm analyzes the results and creates a report showing the rank order of team role skills exhibited by that person. Figure 2.1 shows one such report.

Figure 2.1: Belbin Team Role Report

	Team Roles in Rank Order								
	1	**2**	**3**	**4**	**5**	**6**	**7**	**8**	**9**
Self-perception	**ME**	**CF**	**IMP**	**SH**	**SP**	**CO**	**PL**	**RI**	**TW**
Observer #1	ME	CF	PL	IMP	CO	SP	TW	RI	SH
Observer #2	CF	IMP	PL	ME	CO	SP	SH	TW	RI
Observer #3	CF	ME	CO	SP	IMP	PL	TW	SH	RI
Observer #4	CF	PL	TW	SP	CO	ME	SH	IMP	RI
OVERALL RANKING	CF	ME	PL	IMP	SP	CO	SH	TW	RI

The answers to the self-ratings showed that this person thought they were strongest in the Monitor Evaluator role. Only one of the four Observers also rated that person highest on ME skills; another rated them highly enough in that category that it ended up second overall. Everyone agreed this person did not show strong skill as a Resource Investigator (it fell 8th or 9th on each ranking). The overall ranking of skills for this person is shown at the bottom.

The relative strengths of roles vary from person to person. We have seen Team Role analyses of individuals that show just one very strong role and every other role being very weak. This is unusual but, clearly, not impossible. Most often, there are several roles that a person and his or her observers agree are very prominent, and several roles that emerge as being rather weak, leaving a middle group in which the person is not exceptionally strong or weak. As we examine the composition of teams we often find it convenient to divide the nine roles into three groupings in the following manner:

- The top three ranked skills (overall ranking of one to three) for any person are considered their strengths or **preferred roles**. These behaviors come most easily or naturally to the person and are what they will be best at. The preferred roles for the person shown in Figure 2.1, for example, are Completer Finisher, Monitor Evaluator, and Plant.

- The middle three skills (overall ranking of four through six) are called **manageable**: although performing those team roles doesn't come quite as naturally as preferred skills, the person can often fulfill those roles competently, especially on a short-term or situational basis. For the person in Figure 2.1, they would not naturally show Implementer, Specialist, or Coordinator skills very often if left to their own inclinations, but could do so if the situation called for it.

- The bottom three team roles are related to tasks and attributes that the person is weakest in and are called **least preferred roles**. Asking a person to perform these least preferred roles will put them under great stress. The person in Figure 2.1 would have a very hard time acting as a Shaper, Team Worker, or Resource Investigator, and probably would not perform very well in those roles. Note, as stated above, the division into sets of three must be checked carefully. Some people may have only one or two preferred roles, with more manageable or least preferred roles making up the difference.

The flipside of strengths: Allowable weaknesses

The factors that determine a person's strengths also lead to inherent weaknesses that are unlikely to be changeable in the short or even medium term. Where roles are heavily influenced by personality (e.g., Resource Investigators typically are somewhat to very extroverted), attempts to fix a weakness often serve to destroy the associated strength while having only a slight beneficial impact on the weakness being targeted. Thus attempting to rein in a highly extroverted RI would probably place a strain on that person and harm their ability to network and do the things RIs are good at. We'll talk more about dealing with allowable weaknesses later in this chapter.

Team Applications

The Belbin methodology can be used either proactively (to help shape team composition) or reactively (as a diagnostic tool when the team has its kickoff meeting or later when problems arise). There are many situations in which there is very little opportunity to actually change team composition. In these cases the Belbin approach can be extremely effective in bringing about an awareness of the imbalances that exist. Once team role imbalances are recognized, a team can develop effective strategies to address them.

Roles needed during project phases

Different team roles take on additional significance during different phases of a project. As shown in Table 2.A for example:

- Shaper and Coordinator roles are particularly important when a team is setting direction and establishing customer needs.

- Plant and Resource Investigator roles are critical when coming up with the creative ideas for meeting those needs.

- When a team needs to develop plans, the skills found within the Monitor/Evaluator and Specialist roles are in greatest demand.

- If team success relies on making connections outside the team, the team should call on the Resource Investigator and Team Worker roles.

- Keeping the team organized and on track is best done by the Implementer and/or Coordinator roles.

- To make sure that all plans are carried through to the last detail, the team needs the contributions of the Completer/Finisher and Implementer roles.

Table 2.A: Importance of Roles Varies by Project Phase

Needs	SH	CO
Ideas	PL	RI
Plans	ME	SP
Contacts	RI	TW
Organization	IMP	CO
Follow-through	CF	IMP

Teams that aren't aware of how to match different needs with different team roles often muddle through, calling on anyone in the team to do any kind of work. At best, that approach is inefficient. At worst, it can increase stress and even lead to total failure as people are called on to perform tasks they are ill-suited for.

Interpreting Balance and Imbalance

The other main application of team role knowledge is dealing with imbalances in team composition. Belbin proved that balanced teams perform better over the long run than imbalanced ones. Specifically, what is required is that each of the nine roles is represented on a team. Table 2.A explains why: while at any given point a team's tasks may not require that all nine roles be present, every role is needed over the long haul as a team's needs change. (The potential for temporary success of imbalanced teams was borne out by Belbin's imbalanced "pure teams" which did quite well at selected tasks, but which failed over the longer run.)

Teams may be imbalanced in two ways:

- A role may not be represented on the team (a team role void). The consequence of a team role void is that at some point, the absent role will be in demand and there will be no one filling it. This team's struggles will be quite predictable: For example, if the team lacks someone strong in the Shaper role, it may be slow to action. If it lacks someone strong in the Plant role, it may not develop the best possible strategies.

- A role may be over-represented (a team role surplus), which carries its own pitfalls. These teams will often devolve into internal competition as the members who are strong in the same roles try to outdo one another in the same role. A team filled with individuals who prefer the Plant role, for example, is likely to become immersed in ideas at the expense of addressing practical realities. Creative individuals tend to feel significant ownership of their own ideas and this can often lead to "idea competition." Shaper-heavy teams will argue over goals, and power struggles will quickly break out. Members on surplussed-teams tend to overindulge the activities that are part of the surplus role. In a Plant-heavy team, brainstorming is fun for the team members, so they continue to do it long after the point of diminishing returns. These teams often take on the worst characteristics of the role that is in surplus.

Analyzing a team's balance

To tell whether there are voids or surpluses, the team needs to create a map that compiles the rankings for each team member by filling in a form like that shown in Figure 2.2.

Figure 2.2 Format for Team Role Map

	Team Role	Team Member A	Team Member B	Team Member C	Team Member D
Thinking	Plant				
	Monitor Evaluator				
	Specialist				
Action	Shaper				
	Implementer				
	Completer Finisher				
People	Coordinator				
	Team Worker				
	Resource Investigator				

The results are then analyzed by comparing the ranks of various roles across all team members. One example is shown on the next page (Figure 2.3), along with the conclusions that can be drawn from it.

Figure 2.3: Map of Team Role Rankings

	Person A	Person B	Person C	Person D	Person E	Person F
PL	7	7	2	4	9	8
ME	4	2	4	1	4	2
SP	5	3	5	5	8	1
SH	3	1	1	2	7	3
IMP	8	4	9	8	2	5
CF	1	9	6	7	6	6
RI	6	5	8	9	5	7
TW	2	6	7	6	1	9
CO	9	8	3	3	3	4

This six-person team map shows the Belbin results for a team of six people (labeled A to F in the figure). Person A, for example, had a strong preference for being a Completer Finisher, Team Worker, and Shaper, as shown by the rankings 1, 2, 3 in that column. He or she was weakest in Plant, Implementer, and Coordinator capabilities, as shown by the rankings of 7, 8, 9. Ideally, the team should have at least one 1, 2, or 3 in each of the roles (showing that the role will naturally be represented by someone on the team)—but not too many high numbers for any role.

As can be seen in the map above, there are many 1s, 2s, and 3s in the Shaper role meaning this team has a surplus of those capabilities. Conversely, there are only scores of 5 and lower in the Resource Investigator role; this a void. Left to its own devices, the team would probably have a great deal of Shaper-induced conflict: arguing over direction and goals, struggles amongst the Shapers to lead the meetings and the team, etc. The lack of Resource Investigators could also pose problems in that the team would not have an outward focus. When teams become insular, they can become isolated from other parts of the organization and fail to communicate with or manage their external contacts.

The other roles seem to be fine, with the possible exceptions of Coordinator (CO) and Monitor Evaluator (ME), both of which have borderline team role surpluses. The ME concentration is more problematic than that of CO, due to the higher ranking of the preferred roles (ranks are 1, 2, and 2 for ME versus 3, 3, and 3 for CO). Also, the fact that the lowest ranking for anyone in the ME role is #4 can cause issues. A team with an ME surplus would tend toward over-analysis, potentially leading to paralysis by analysis. In this particular team, paralysis is probably unlikely to occur because the Shapers would quickly become impatient for results.

Dealing with imbalances

Only about 10% of teams will be balanced perfectly (no voids, no surpluses, each role having at least one high rank), assuming that they are made up of six randomly chosen members.

The good news is that the remaining 90% of the teams that are formed without considering role balance and which have some structural issues can almost all be made effective. There are a few cases (roughly 5% of the time), where the team is so imbalanced that a change in membership may be the only way to adequately restore balance in the team.

Addressing voids: Determine which team member has the missing role as a manageable one (that is, it ranks 4, 5, or 6 in the assessment). Thereafter, when that role is needed, that individual will have to stretch beyond their preferred roles to fill the scarce one. This should be sustainable, provided that role is not required to be played on a continual basis. Normally, in project teams this will not be an issue as the team will meet infrequently, and the person making the "sacrifice" will have ample opportunity outside of these meetings to revert to more preferred roles. A key success factor in this strategy is that the rest of the team recognize that the person may be stretching beyond their comfort zone, and be supportive, perhaps by taking on some of the person's other workload, etc.

Dealing with surpluses: Surpluses are more difficult to deal with than voids. In some cases, it will be sufficient for the team members with a preference for the surplus role to merely throttle back their attempts to play it. This will often work in situations where the team members are not deeply emotionally involved in the debate. However, this is often difficult as the preferred role feels good or fun; as a result it is very hard to not indulge it. A more successful strategy is often for the team to firmly establish one or two of the members who will play the lead role for the surplus team role. It will then be necessary for the others with that preferred role to consciously avoid it completely, often by focusing on playing another of their preferred or manageable team roles. It may also be necessary for the team to empower one member of the team who does not have the surplus role as a preferred role to be the monitor of team activity and to "raise the flag" when the team has inadvertently devolved into unproductive indulgence of that role.

Balancing in action

Returning to the mortgage team example, Irene's mortgage service design team had their Belbin reports generated. They discovered that three of the members—Irene, Carlos, and Roger— all have Plant as a preferred role while Sandy is a strong Completer/Finisher. Irene is also a strong Resource Investigator; Carlos and Roger are both strong in the Specialist team role (though in different areas, fortunately). None on the team are strong in Shaper tendencies.

Given this team composition, it is not surprising that the team bogged down in the design phase, when the **surplus of Plant** tendencies dominated. The three most assertive members of the team were unwilling to leave behind the creative phase. This problem was exacerbated by the **void of a Shaper**, which meant there was no one who would plunge a stake in the ground and say "Let's just do it."

It was impractical to add new people to the team at this point, so the team discussed other options for getting past the problem areas. To get out of the idea churn from being Plant-heavy, Irene did her best to fill the Shaper role when *required, pushing the team towards action. Roger also focused on his Implementer role, helping them get out of the design phase and into planning.*

To reduce the stress on team members who were required to play their manageable or even least-preferred roles, the team set up a ground rule that acknowledged which roles were missing on the team, encouraging them all to try to notice when that role was needed, and to step in to fill it as necessary.

The situation faced by this team is typical of what you'll encounter on your own teams. There will likely be too many people strong in a few roles and not enough who are strong in other roles. In some cases, the best recourse is to change team membership so that all roles are represented, but as noted above that is not always possible or even necessary.

The best strategy overall is to acknowledge which roles are missing and decide who will fill those voids. Look first at people for whom the roles are manageable; as a last resort turn to someone for whom the role falls into the least preferred category.

Often, just the awareness of having a surplus of one role will help deal with the issue of having too many team members making similar contributions. Having a number of Plants, for instance, may not be a problem if there is an explicit plan to deal with the idea competitiveness on the team that is often present when there is a surplus of Plants. Our experience suggests that teams need to make sure their vigilance against the offending behavior must be maintained or it may subtly creep back as individuals revert to their usual patterns of behavior.

Individual Applications

There are several ramifications of Belbin's research for individuals as well as teams. The three primary impacts for the individual lie in self-management:

- **Role-playing:** what is the best team role to play in a certain setting
- **Coherence**: making sure that how you see yourself matches how others see you
- **Allowable weaknesses**: how to handle the weaknesses that are the flipside of strengths for each team role

Role-playing

Role-playing is a situational exercise conducted at the individual level. As we saw from the team mapping discussion above, there are certain situations in which it may be advisable or even essential for the individual to shift away from his or her preferred roles. However, Belbin's advice to individuals is that this should be the exception rather than the rule. The general rule is to play to your strengths (preferred roles should be sought out), and avoid your weaknesses (least preferred roles should be delegated to others).

The reasoning behind this advice is that, to a great degree, an individual's preferred team roles are rooted in deeply embedded behavior patterns. While the need for various roles on the team will change over time and team members will have to shift between their preferred (and perhaps even manageable) roles, the reality is that at any point in time a person is most likely to be successful if they are engaged in activities that play to their strengths and make their weaknesses irrelevant.

What typically occurs when we stray into our least preferred roles is that we set ourselves up for failure or at the very least take on a great deal of stress with the likelihood of achieving mediocre results. Attempts to play the weaker roles often come across poorly to the rest of the team as well, leading to lowered trust and increased interpersonal conflict. Stress is a feeling of anxiety based in being unable to cope with a situation. This definition seems to line up nicely with what Belbin's least preferred roles represent. Asking a non-Plant to be creative and unorthodox will be unlikely to generate much creativity but will almost certainly put that individual on the spot and under stress.

Once you know your own team role preferences, it is your responsibility to actively seek out opportunities where your strengths will be valued contributions and to manage situations so that you are not requested or required to act in areas where you are weak. (The basic formula suggested by Belbin's research maximizes both an individual's contribution to team success and the individual's own personal success.)

It is also your responsibility to be alert for situations when you need to shift between roles. In our mortgage team, for example, Irene realized that she had to temporarily abandon one of her preferred roles, that of Plant, in order to allow the team to make progress. Roger did the same thing, focusing on where he could contribute in an Implementer role and suppressing his natural Plant capabilities.

Coherence

Coherence is the degree to which you see yourself as others see you. This attribute is almost universally present in people identified as great leaders. It is embodied in adjectives commonly used to describe admired leaders like genuine, authentic, transparent, self-aware, mature, consistent. Coherence more strongly correlates with effective leadership than any of the nine team roles—meaning that the role which a person plays is less important than how well that person knows and plays to their strengths and manages their weaknesses.

Having coherence makes it very easy to accurately place a person into suitable tasks; no guessing is required. Also, coherent individuals are generally viewed as easy to deal with because they are predictable and consistent. At an interpersonal level, coherence allows other people to more quickly understand who we are and avoid inadvertently offending us because our true nature is more quickly and consistently visible.

The benefit to an individual of becoming more coherent is that more of the time in the workplace will be spent on tasks to which they are well-suited. This will naturally allow them to shine more frequently and garner rewards and recognition. On the other side, they will more often avoid tasks to which they are ill-suited, thereby avoiding career- or reputation-damaging incidents.

Allowable Weaknesses

That weaknesses exist is obvious; what may be less obvious is whether the weakness is "allowable", in the sense that the team or individual should accept the weakness and find ways to counteract it through other roles on the team, or if it is "disallowable" and the person needs to find a way to change that counterproductive behavior.

Judging this issue depends on what impact the weakness will have on the team and whether compensations can be made for it. The absent-mindedness that may accompany creativity in the Plant role can be compensated for by other roles' strengths, for instance the detail-oriented Completer Finisher role. It is a matter of degrees: If the person over-indulges the Plant role and forgets to come to a meeting, that would be disallowable. But merely becoming lost in thought and distracted during a meeting would usually be permissible.

Generally, the weaknesses attached to preferred team roles should be accepted, but consciously managed by the person so that it does not become disallowable. The worst approach is often to try to fix or eliminate the weakness completely; this merely kills the flowers along with the weeds. Often the best way to manage a weakness will involve seeking out a complementary role in another person that inherently offsets the weakness and trying to work collaboratively with that person so that the weakness never impedes the progress of the team.

Does Belbin knowledge really make a difference?

Quite often, the insights gained from a Belbin analysis have a profound effect on people. As proof, we offer the following real-life case studies (names of people and companies have been changed for privacy reasons):

Case #1: Nick

Nick was a middle-aged manager who had a lot of experience in project management and a very successful career. Though he had good people skills in general, he had noticed over the years that there were occasional disconnects within the teams he led. By profession he was an accountant, which required him to be very focused and detail-oriented. But by career path he was now a manager, required to be very strategic in his thinking.

Team members sometimes thought of Nick as micromanaging because he'd try to take over anything analytical. He'd often take on a lot of tasks because he was "the boss." At the same time, the team knew he wasn't the greatest at following through on details, so sometimes tasks would not get done on time.

Nick's perception of himself was as a "super" performer in the Monitor Evaluator role, always thinking strategically, looking at options, making shrewd judgments about how to get work done. He thought that one of his weakest skills was at the creative end, in what Belbin classifies as a Plant.

To his surprise, other people's perceptions were almost the exact opposite: they rated him as mediocre or moderate at best in Monitor Evaluator skills and very high in the Plant abilities. (Everything else in his report aligned between his self-perception and the perception of others; the difference in ME and PL scoring was the only glaring discordance.)

This was an "aha" moment for Nick. The more he thought about it, the more he realized that other people's perceptions were more accurate than his own. He really wasn't that good at the kind of patience and attention required to be good at the Monitor Evaluator role. And conversely, he really enjoyed the divergent thinking associated with the Plant role.

Over the next year, Nick focused very deliberately on developing his creative side. At first, he even asked his teammates to tell him when he was being creative so he could start to recognize his own Plant-ness (so to speak). Coupled with his good people skills, it turned out his true strengths were in the roles of Plant, Resource Investigator, and Coordinator. Therefore he would come up with creative ideas, not only on his own but also by making connections with many other people, as is typical of an RI. His Coordinator skills were very useful in the early stages of a project, when it was critical that the team get organized around what it needed to accomplish.

Nick learned that he really needed to be paired with individuals who could play the Completer Finisher and Implementer roles effectively if anything was going to get done well and on time! He also became adept at switching roles: serving on a team that happened to have a lot of Coordinators and Plants, he would even slip into his fourth strongest role, Team Worker—meaning he would not try to take control as much as make sure that everyone got a chance to contribute.

As the year passed, Nick realized that his teams were working together better than ever before, achieving improved results with greater contributions from all involved. Nick also found that his workday was much less stressful. And he's never looked back from there.

Case #2: June

In some ways, June's story is the opposite of Nick's. When she went through the Belbin analysis, it turned out she had a very coherent report: that the way she perceived herself was the same way that others perceived her—as having strong Implementer role skills. There was one slight difference however: other people also recognized that her strong people skills would be an asset in the Coordinator role, but that wasn't something June had ever thought she could do. Individuals who are strong in the Coordinator role are often leaders within a group, whether formally or informally, and have a certain confidence that allows them to fulfill that role well.

As June thought about this more, she realized that her contentment with gravitating to the Implementer role was limiting her career. In order to grow professionally and personally, she decided she would muscle up the nerve to try performing the Coordinator role. She began being more deliberate and assertive in making sure the pieces of her teams meshed well together. She flourished in this new role, taking on more and more leadership responsibilities over time.

Case #3: Pete

Pete had a meteoric career in sales, quickly rising to the top and staying there for a number of years. Another company recognized his success by offering him the chance to manage sales in one of its divisions. Pete jumped at the chance for career advancement. He approached his new job with enthusiasm, eager to prove himself an able leader.

Unfortunately, things didn't go well. After a few months, his division had fallen to having the worst sales performance of any in the company. Because Pete's total compensation was heavily tied to the division's sales performance, he was now making less than half of his income at his previous employer. The future was looking quite bleak when Pete had the chance to attend a Belbin seminar. That's when the light bulbs began coming on.

He realized that he had been equating "leadership" with what Belbin called the Coordinator role—which was one of his weakest areas. He had far too short an attention span, did not really enjoy detailed follow-up, and tended to dominate meetings. That was why his team was constantly behind and people felt they weren't given a chance to contribute.

One of Pete's first moves when he returned to the office was to hire an individual who was strong in the Coordinator role as his second-in-command. With that person in place and playing the CO role, Pete focused more on what he did well, connecting with resources and opportunistically pursuing new leads (the RI role). In a remarkably short time, his team's performance made a complete turnaround, becoming the most successful division in the company. Pete returned to a happier worklife, and his income more than tripled from its low point.

Conclusion

As you've just seen, knowledge of Belbin strengths and weaknesses can have a huge effect on both your own personal and professional development and on the success of your teams. Initiating a project without consideration of team composition is a classic failure mode seen throughout companies today. The Belbin Team Role Theory can be applied to both diagnose existing teams and to design new ones from scratch. It is the diagnosis and identification of countermeasures that lie at the heart of consistently successful project teams and project leaders. It has been our experience that projects can be shortened by the judicious use of team composition techniques because it eliminates wasted effort or indecision, to say nothing of improved quality of results or the more positive experiences of the team members.

APPENDIX 1

Team Roles

Quick Reference Guide

Plant

Contribution

People who are strong in the Plant role are innovators and inventors and can be highly creative. They provide the seeds and ideas from which major developments spring. Usually, they prefer to operate by themselves at some distance from the other members of the team, using their imagination and often working in an unorthodox manner. They tend to be introverted and react strongly to criticism and praise. Their ideas may often be radical and may overlook practicalities.

They are independent, clever, and original. They may be weak in communicating with other people, especially those who are not as cerebral as they are.

Role on a Team

The main contribution of the Plant team role is to generate new proposals and to solve complex problems. The Plant role is often needed in the initial stages of a project or when a project is failing to progress. This role is prone to divergent or tangential lines of reasoning which can be counterproductive in some settings.

The Plant role in action

Showing strengths

During a product strategy meeting, Norma sits and listens as two vice presidents argue over which of two products the sales force should focus on selling. One VP supports Product A because of its greater initial profitability. The other supports Product B because early marketing reports show a lot of potential though its costs are expected to be higher. The two argue back and forth for some time. Norma appears indifferent, doodling on her notepad. Finally one of the VPs addresses her. "Norma, are you paying attention? What do you think?"

Norma puts down her pen. "Yes, I've been listening. And it occurs to me that maybe we're missing something," she says. "I think if we reconfigured our production lines, we could redistribute our overhead costs and sell both product A and B more profitably without overburdening our sales force. The three dive into the numbers and production strategies more deeply and realize that Norma is right.

> COMMENT: This is typical Plant behavior, listening closely to data and arguments (even if it doesn't look like they are!), and getting their minds around the issues before coming up with a new idea that hadn't occurred to anyone else.

Showing a weakness

At a later meeting, Norma and the two vice presidents are presenting their recommendation to the president of their division. He starts peppering Norma with questions: "What timeframe are we looking at to make these changes? What will it take to get it done? Is this really practical?"

Norma can't answer any of those questions. She loves the creative work, but loses interest once the talk focuses on how to get something done.

> COMMENT: Though some people who are strong in the Plant role also have Implementer tendencies, most don't pay much attention to practical issues like feasibility or deadlines. That's allowable as long as you have someone on the team who does care about those issues.

Monitor Evaluator

Contribution

Strength in this role requires a serious-minded, prudent approach with a built-in immunity from being over-enthusiastic. This can slow down decision-making. High critical-thinking ability is a requirement for this role as well as an ability to take all factors into consideration. .

Role on a Team

This role contributes by analyzing problems and evaluating ideas and suggestions, weighing the pros and cons of different options.

The Monitor Evaluator role in action

Showing strengths

A strategic team is discussing the idea of consolidating office locations. Three of the participants are very enthusiastic, seeing a wealth of possibilities for saving on overhead and achieving other efficiencies. The plans are well underway when Marty speaks up.

> *"Hold on everybody,"* he says, *"I think we're getting way ahead of ourselves."* There's sudden quiet in the room and the energy level drops precipitously. *"It seems like you're gung-ho on closing the Sullivan office, but that's also the home of our biggest customer and we have those tax incentives from the city. I don't think they're going to be too happy about that. We really need to explore some more options here before making a decision."*

The rest of the team immediately saw that Marty was

right in his assessment. Though disappointed at having to reassess their options, they realized it was good thing he'd stopped them before they got too far down the line.

COMMENT: Those who contribute the most strongly in the Monitor Evaluator role have an eye towards the larger strategic picture surrounding decisions and want to get a lot of information before making a final call.

Showing a weakness

At the next meeting of this team, one of the team members reports that she's talked to the customer and moving the office wouldn't be a big deal to them. But Marty shows them data on the impact of losing the tax incentive for those operations, and its much bigger than anyone anticipated. Still, the team decides to go ahead with the consolidation. Marty's reaction: "When this goes bust, don't blame me."

COMMENT: Those adept at the Monitor Evaluator role can have a tendency to sound skeptical (if not cynical). Marty's team had learned to appreciate his strategic insights and ignore his occasional negative attitude.

Specialist

Contribution

Typically individuals who excel at the Specialist role are dedicated and pride themselves on acquiring technical skills and specialized knowledge. Their priorities focus on maintaining professional standards and on furthering and defending their own field. Eventually, they become an expert by sheer commitment along a narrow front.

As managers, they command support because they know more about their subject than anyone else and can usually be called upon to make decisions based on in-depth experience. While they show great pride in their own subject, they may lack interest in other people's subjects.

Role on a Team

This role plays an indispensable part in some teams. It provides the rare skill or knowledge that is key to fixing the problem being addressed.

A Specialist in action

Showing strengths

The site review council at a dialysis clinic is reviewing data on patient performance over the past months. The nurses are telling the team about problems that some patients are having with the traditional "ports" used to access arm veins for the dialysis treatment.

At that point, Lee pipes up: "I just saw a report in the latest nursing journals where they were testing a new device for accessing veins through the chest. I did more research, and it appears this new device is legit. Maybe we should invite one of the reps here and see if it would work for those patients."

> COMMENT: *Those adept at this role often pride themselves in being expert in an area of their choosing. Though not always focused on the team's immediate needs, they must be allowed time to explore their discipline because someday that knowledge will come in handy.*

Showing a weakness

After a presentation by the company rep for the new device, Lee has become a strong advocate. When the rest of the team wants to proceed cautiously and even visit other clinics where the device is being used, she thinks that extra effort is a waste of time. "I know what I'm talking about here," she complains. "Why don't you trust me?"

> COMMENT: *Individuals who are strong in the Specialist role can tend to view the world through their narrow lens of expertise. They can sometimes get so enamored of what they're doing that they fail to see the larger picture, and may resent having their ideas questioned.*

Shaper

Contribution

The Shaper role is associated with high levels of motivation, a lot of nervous energy and a strong need for achievement. If obstacles arise, this role is required to find a way around them.

Role on a Team

This role is required to drive forward progress. As the name implies, this contribution shapes group discussion or activities.

The Shaper Role in action

Showing strengths

Bill leads the acquisition department in a financial services firm. He was becoming frustrated with his team. A new deal was in the works, but the advisory team couldn't seem to come to a decision. Norm was still manning the phones, surfacing alternative acquisition targets for the team to explore. Ellen was trying to map out the proposed acquisition in excruciating detail.

Bill stepped in to call a halt to all of the meandering. He knew the company had to grow or they would be gobbled up themselves. Two days after this intervention, Bill had lined up all the financing, gotten corporate approval, and was ready to take the plunge.

Showing a weakness

The acquisition looks like it's a go, but in the final meeting, Ellen keeps raising practical issues for the team to explore. "Given the other three deals we have in the pipeline, I just want to make sure this is the best use of our resources," she says.

This is the last straw for Bill. "I'm really losing patience with this!" he yells. "We have looked at this acquisition every which way from Sunday. Stop dinking around, Ellen. We would have this deal done by now if it weren't for you."

> COMMENT: *Individuals who are adept at this role are often impatient and can be abrasive since they don't fear controversy. It's allowable that they act this way, but that doesn't give them license to ride roughshod over others. In fact, in this case, Bill later apologized to Ellen and the rest of the team, explaining that his anxiety around getting the deal done had gotten the better of him. He acknowledged that Ellen had some good points around resource usage, and the team had some productive discussions on that issue.*

Implementer

Contribution

Executing this role requires practical common sense and a good deal of self-control, discipline, and an ability to tackle problems in a systematic fashion. On a wider front this role requires high levels of reliability and a capacity for applied action.

Individuals who execute this role effectively can be seen to lack spontaneity and show signs of rigidity.

Role on a Team

The Implementer role is necessary to keep the team focused on what needs to be done. An aptitude for establishing project plans and anticipating barriers that need to be addressed is required.

The Implementer role in action

Showing strengths

Maxwell Accounting Systems is considering the purchase of a major new contact management software package. The CFO has already made the decision to go ahead with the purchase and is meeting with the head IT guy and Carlotta, who will be in charge of the conversion project.

At the beginning of the meeting, Carlotta points out a potential roadblock to the others. "Did you realize that you set the purchase date just two months ahead of when we're moving the offices?" she asks. Juan, the CFO, chimes in. "I'm not clear why that's a problem. Two months is plenty of time to get the new system up and running, and it won't be affected by the move."

"You're right," answers Carlotta, "but I've seen the master moving plan and about half the people in every department are going to be tied up a good 6 to 8 weeks before the move—and those are the same people we need to support the software upgrade. I think it will overlap too much."

> COMMENT: The Implementer role provides the team with a person who always has an eye on the practical aspects of any decision, "What will it take to make this work?"

Showing a weakness

Juan, Carlotta, and the IT head honcho decided to move the purchase date for the new contact management program until two weeks after the big move. As they begin fleshing out the details of the changeover, it's clear that Carlotta is increasingly uncomfortable. "You know," she says, "we've been using Lotus Notes for about seven years now and it seems to work fine. Are you sure the change will help us?"

> COMMENT: The orientation that makes individuals successful at filling the Implementer role can also be accompanied by some inflexibility and an aversion to the uncertainty and risk of trying something new.

Completer Finisher

Contribution

This role represents people who have a great capacity for follow-through and attention to detail. Individuals who excel at this role may be motivated by internal anxiety and are not often keen on delegating, preferring to tackle all tasks themselves.

In management they excel by the high standards to which they aspire and by their concern for precision, attention to detail, and follow-through.

Role on a Team

This role is essential when there are tasks that demand close concentration and a high degree of accuracy.

The Completer Finisher role in action

Showing strengths

The product design team couldn't survive without Peter. His attention to detail was famous companywide. He would test and re-test and test again each product feature. While this sometimes slowed down development, it was well known that any product he had touched would launch perfectly. Everybody wants Peter on their team because they know they can rely on him to get his assignments done completely.

> COMMENT: *This role is essential to any team facing a need for high quality. Having this role filled effectively will enable the team to execute plans to the tiniest detail, meeting high standards of performance at every step.*

Showing a weakness

During the development of one product, new information came to light that affected the design of a feature that Peter was responsible for. The requested change really put him back. "But we've already tested everything and it works perfectly. We can't change things now. It would mess up everything." The team leader suggests that if Peter doesn't want to handle the change, perhaps someone else on the team could step in. "No way," says Peter. "This is my baby. I know how this works better than anyone else."

COMMENT: *Some degree of perfectionism is not only expected but desirable in those executing the Completer Finisher role. It's that attention to detail that everyone comes to rely on.*

Resource Investigator

Contribution

This role brings a lot of energy to the team. Those that execute this role well are often enthusiastic, extroverted, and quick to act. They are good at communicating with people both inside and outside the company. Although not necessarily a great source of original ideas, bringing to the team other people's ideas and developing them is the function they fulfill. As the name suggests, they are skilled at finding out what is available and bringing it back to the team. Being inquisitive is an asset in this role.

Role on a Team

This role requires an ability and interest in exploring and reporting back on ideas, developments or resources outside the team.

The Resource Investigator role in action

Showing strengths

The accounts payable team was really on the hot seat. Customer complaints about invoice and payment problems had been rising for months, and nothing they'd tried had worked. They'd upgraded their training, redesigned some software interface screens, but to little effect. Then one day Jamal came in very excited. "I was at a Rotary meeting last night and ran into Mark, one of the guys over at Maxwell Accounting. I was chatting with him about our low ratings and asked if he had any insights he could offer. He said our recent changes in product codes were causing lots of headaches at their end. Orders were getting messed up, which meant they had to ask for return authorizations and credit vouchers.

"On my way in this morning," continued Jamal, "I stopped by Derek's office and got his input on the code changes, then asked him to come talk to the whole team. I think we can brainstorm some ways to make our internal changes completely invisible to the customer."

> *COMMENT: Those that excel at the Resource Investigator role are typically the ultimate networkers. They just naturally foster connections with lots of people, and will use those connections to help identify solutions to problems and to draw in expertise when the team needs it. They are the people most likely to make sure that viewpoints from stakeholders outside the team are represented during discussions and decision making.*

Showing a weakness

Back at his desk after the meeting with Derek and his team, Jamal gets a call from a colleague in another department. "Where's that report you promised me yesterday?" asks the colleague. "It slipped my mind," confesses Jamal. "I got this great insight for solving this complaint problem we've been having and spent the morning working on that."

> *COMMENT: The strengths that we have been describing for this role can often be accompanied by certain weaknesses. It's not unusual to see some slippage in meeting commitments. While this is allowable to some degree, those in the RI role should find ways to get reminders about less-exciting commitments (like doing reports) so they don't let down customers or coworkers who may be depending on their work to make their own deadlines.*

Team Worker

Contribution

This role is characterized by a great capacity for flexibility and for adapting to different situations and people. Being perceptive and diplomatic are attributes that are required to fulfill this role. Good listening skills are important as is the ability to work with sensitivity with others on the team.

Role on a Team

The impact on the team of having this role executed effectively is that team morale tends to be better and people seem to cooperate better. Their role is to prevent interpersonal problems from festering within a team and thus allowing all team members to contribute effectively.

The Team Worker role in action

Showing strengths

Gerry and Helen were really going at it. Gerry thought Helen was ignoring customer data by suggesting the team go with an option for using a cheaper material in the product design. Helen thought Gerry was being naïve about what the company could afford in product cost. Each was on the verge of stalking out of the meeting when Keith stepped in.

"You know," said Keith, "I think you both have some good points here. Gerry's right that we have to be careful not to go with a cheaper material if it's going to harm the structural integrity. But Helen's right that we have very firm price targets for this product and our profit margins will be too low if we spend too much on materials. I think there's a way we could go with the more expensive material without harming the potential profit margin."

> COMMENT: As the name implies, those that fill this role are inherently concerned that the team works well as a unit. They will always be looking for ways to smooth over tense situations while making sure that all viewpoints are acknowledged.

Showing a weakness

Keith was glad that his suggestions for moving beyond the conflict between Helen and Gerry was accepted by the team. He clearly remembered a meeting not long ago when something similar happened, only this time Helen put him on the spot, asking him to choose sides between two alternatives suggested for the design of another element. He was extremely uncomfortable, not wanting to offend anyone's feelings, and hemmed and hawed until Helen gave up trying to make him take a stance.

> COMMENT: Sometimes the strengths we have described are accompanied by a discomfort with conflict. Obviously, that feeds into their strength in wanting to seek harmony, but it isn't allowable as a mechanism to avoid dealing with the source of the conflict. Doing so blocks progress because the issues go underground and may not be addressed.

Coordinator

Contribution

Teams need individuals who are quick to spot individuals' talents and to use them in the pursuit of group objectives. Those that do a good job at the Coordinator role are well placed when put in charge of a team of people with diverse skills and personal characteristics. Their motto might well be "consultation with control" and they usually believe in tackling problems calmly. Mature, trusting and confident, they delegate readily. In some organizations, this role can clash with that of Shaper.

Role on a Team

The distinguishing feature of the Coordinator role is the ability to motivate others to work towards shared goals. While not necessarily the cleverest members of a team, Coordinators have a broad outlook and generally command respect.

The Coordinator role in action

Showing strengths

The HR team at a small company had the potential to be fractious. One member had been with the company for fifteen years and was happy with the way things were. Another member was new to the company and brimming with suggestions of ways to do things differently.

Oscar, the HR manager and team leader, knew it was his job to make sure everyone had a chance to contribute. He established a ground rule for the team that they would always be open to hearing new ideas, and that the team would always strive for consensus around major decisions. During meetings, he'd occasionally rein in the enthusiasm of the new guy, while at the same time making sure the most senior employee got her say. By maintaining impartiality, he was able to steer the team towards effective decisions without appearing to take sides. He also kept on top of when the team would need other resources, such as experts in the various areas of benefits (healthcare, retirement plans, vacation, etc.), and always made sure that the right people were in the room together.

> COMMENT: *Those adept in this role are very skilled at building cohesion on a team. They don't usually try to persuade people directly, but rather shape the meeting or discussion process so consensus emerges over time and people convince themselves of what the best options are. They are good at managing resources and coordinating actions so that handoffs between people work seamlessly.*

Showing a weakness

When it came time to draft a new retirement plan, Oscar let Tim, the new guy, take the lead, asking him to work with an external retirement plan specialist to develop a draft proposal for the whole team to review. He intended to check in with Tim a few times a week, but often got distracted by all other tasks. Then he got a call one day from the external specialist, "Listen, Oscar, you know I'm happy to help out, but I think Tim is asking me to make decisions that really you should be making. I think you'd be happier with the result if you were more involved at this stage."

> COMMENT: *In filling the Coordinator role which requires keeping many balls in play, attention to detail may suffer. Sometimes other team members may feel that delegation has morphed into abdication. Clarifying expectations up front may help to obviate these situations.*

APPENDIX 2

Interpreting a Belbin Report

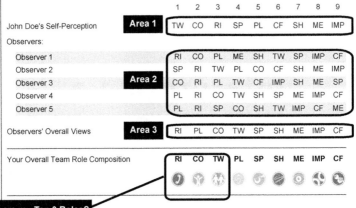

BELBIN

John Doe

Analysis of your Team Role Composition

This report provides an overview of Team Roles as seen by yourself and others, in order from most prominent (column 1) to least (column 9). Your overall Team Role composition is not simply an average of each individual line, but a weighted integration of your perceptions and your Observers' views, which takes many factors into account.

This report is based on your Self-Perception plus 5 Observer Assessments.

		1	2	3	4	5	6	7	8	9
John Doe's Self-Perception	**Area 1**	TW	CO	RI	SP	PL	CF	SH	ME	IMP
Observers:										
Observer 1		RI	CO	PL	ME	SH	TW	SP	IMP	CF
Observer 2		SP	RI	TW	PL	CO	CF	SH	ME	IMP
Observer 3	**Area 2**	CO	RI	PL	TW	CF	IMP	SH	ME	SP
Observer 4		PL	RI	CO	TW	SH	SP	ME	IMP	CF
Observer 5		PL	RI	SP	CO	SH	TW	IMP	CF	ME
Observers' Overall Views	**Area 3**	RI	PL	CO	TW	SP	SH	ME	IMP	CF
Your Overall Team Role Composition		RI	CO	TW	PL	SP	SH	ME	IMP	CF

What are my Top 3 Roles?

Whilst there is general agreement between your own views and those of your observers as to your Team Role strengths, there are also some discrepancies. If you feel strongly that you have more to offer in the Team Roles you have identified, it is up to you to declare your preferences in these areas.

Page 3: Analysis of Your Team Role Composition

How to Read This Page

Lists the nine roles in rank order from 1 = strongest to 9 = weakest in three groupings:

SELF (Area 1) - The top line is based only on your own responses to the self-assessment form.

OBSERVERS (Area 2) - The following lines translate each observer's responses into the roles they see you playing. Observer names have been included to provide context for the results, but the raw data of their responses is hidden from you. (You cannot tell if they said you were "professional", "confrontational", fussy", etc.)

OVERALL (Area 3) - The overall ranking is basically a weighted average of all the lines above as calculated by very complex formulas within the Belbin software system. It is over-weighted towards the observers on the premise that they are more accurate than you may be about yourself.

Areas to Investigate

Use the next page to determine how many top roles you have (usually roles 1-4 on the Overall ranking).

Generally, it is preferable for the top roles to always fall in the top half for all the observers, as this indicates consistency in behavior. The greater the agreement across and among the observers, the more consistently your behavior is being perceived.

BELBIN

John Doe
Team Role Overview

> The bar graph in this report shows your Team Roles in order from highest to lowest, using all available information. The other pages of your report will analyse your Team Role Overview in more detail.

This report is based on your Self-Perception plus 5 Observer Assessments.

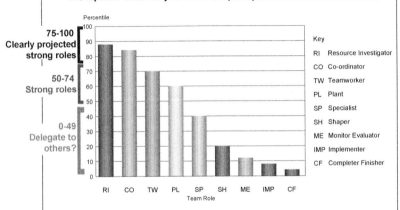

75-100 Clearly projected strong roles	**Key**	
	RI	Resource Investigator
	CO	Co-ordinator
50-74 Strong roles	TW	Teamworker
	PL	Plant
	SP	Specialist
0-49 Delegate to others?	SH	Shaper
	ME	Monitor Evaluator
	IMP	Implementer
	CF	Completer Finisher

The graph above shows your Team Roles in order of preference. Some people have an even spread of Team Roles whilst others may have one or two very high and very low Team Roles. An individual does not necessarily show all nine Team Role behaviours.

This graph is a combination of your views and those of your Observers. When we combine all the information together, we take account of how closely your perception of yourself agrees with others' views of you. Many factors are taken into account when deriving your final Team Role composition.

Page 4: Team Role Overview

How to Read This Page

This page shows your OVERALL team role data in a percentile format, which compares your aptitude for each role compared to the population at large.

A percentile score of 75 or higher is a good indication of you clearly projecting a preferred role. Roles with scores of 50 to 74 may be preferred roles that are not as consistently or strongly projected as they could be. Roles with scores below 50 represent tasks that you should consider delegating to others who can do them better or more easily than you can.

Areas to Investigate

First, identify your top roles. If you don't have any, then look at your best manageable roles and see if any of them can be played more strongly and thereby converted into a top role.

The intent of playing roles more strongly is not to get one or more roles to 100, but to ensure that they are distinctly stronger than other roles. This will allow those you work with to get a better feel for your strengths so you can work better together.

If all the scores are relatively equal to each other, this may indicate that the observers are not getting a clear picture of what your preferred roles are.

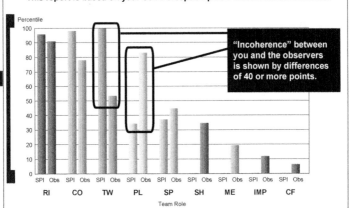

BELBIN®

John Doe
Comparing Self and Observer Perceptions

The bar graph in this report shows how you perceive your Team Role contributions, in comparison to your Observers' views. The table below the graph shows the percentile scores for Self-Perception and Observers.

This report is based on your Self-Perception plus 5 Observer Assessments.

Area 1

"Incoherence" between you and the observers is shown by differences of 40 or more points.

Percentile (y-axis: 0 to 100)

Team Role (x-axis): RI, CO, TW, PL, SP, SH, ME, IMP, CF — each with SPI and Obs

Area 2

Key		Self-Perception (SPI) (Percentile)	Observations (Obs) (Percentile)
RI	Resource Investigator	96	91
CO	Co-ordinator	98	78
TW	Teamworker	100	53
PL	Plant	34	83
SP	Specialist	37	45
SH	Shaper	0	35
ME	Monitor Evaluator	0	19
IMP	Implementer	0	12
CF	Completer Finisher	0	6

Page 5: Comparing Self and Observer Perceptions

How to Read This Page

This page compares the SELF (labeled "SPI") and OBSERVER (labeled "Obs") perceptions of what roles the report subject is playing.

The bar chart (Area 1) displays the data graphically while the underlying numeric data is shown at the bottom of the page (Area 2).

Areas to Investigate

Test for coherence by comparing the two columns of figures at the bottom of the page. If you notice differences of 40 or more (in either direction), these are "disconnects" and indicate a potential lack of coherence (meaning you see yourself significantly differently from how others see you). In the example at left, the roles TW (see comparison "A"), and PL ("B") have differences of 40 or more points.

BELBIN®

John Doe
Your Team Role Preferences

This report shows your percentile scores for each Team Role, according to your Self-Perception responses. Team Roles are divided by percentile score into Preferred, Manageable and Least Preferred Roles.

This report is based upon your Self-Perception only.

Least Preferred Roles	Manageable Roles	Preferred Roles	Team Roles
0 10 20	30 40 50 60	70 80 90 100	
	X		Plant
		X	Resource Investigator
		X	Co-ordinator
X			Shaper
X			Monitor Evaluator
		X	Teamworker
X			Implementer
X			Completer Finisher
	X		Specialist

Points dropped: 0 out of 80

Page 6: Your Team Role Preferences

How to Read This Page

This page is based only on the SELF assessment responses; no observer data has been used. It converts your responses into a score for each role on a scale from 0 to 100.

The scale is based on how your responses compare to those of everyone else in the Belbin software database. A score of 100 would indicate that you gave yourself more points for that role than anyone else in the database, a score of 0 would indicate that no one else was lower than you.

The page is divided somewhat arbitrarily into three sections which correspond to preferred, manageable, and least preferred roles. It is generally preferable to have a few roles in each of the three sections. A profile that has all nine roles clustered right down the middle may indicate that you have an indistinct view of your strengths and weaknesses from a Belbin Team Role standpoint.

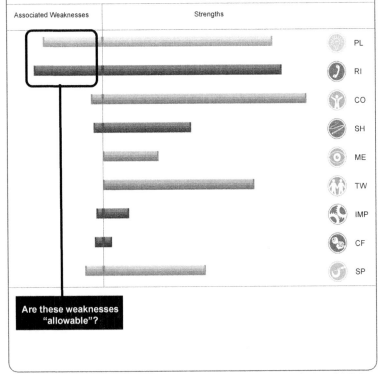

BELBIN®

John Doe

Observed Team Role Strengths and Weaknesses

The bar graph in this report shows your Observers' responses broken down into the strengths and associated weaknesses for each Team Role. An associated weakness is termed allowable if it operates alongside the observed strengths of the Team Role.

This report is based on 5 Observer Assessments.

Associated Weaknesses	Strengths	
		PL
		RI
		CO
		SH
		ME
		TW
		IMP
		CF
		SP

Are these weaknesses "allowable"?

Page 7: Observed Team Role Strengths and Weaknesses

How to Read This Page

This page is based only on the OBSERVER responses. The report totals up all of the observer responses which correspond to the various roles and displays the results as a series of bar graphs.

Each bar is composed of a positive and a negative component. If you look at the page horizontally, positive attributes are shown to the right of the green vertical line indicated by the line labeled "1," negatives to the left of it.

The overall length of any given bar (both the positive and negative components combined) represents HOW MUCH you are seen to play that role. The ratio of positive to negative components within any given bar represents how adept you are at playing that role. It shows HOW WELL the role is being played.

Areas to Investigate

Test for disallowable weaknesses by examining the ratio of positive to negative in each bar. If the ratio is less than 3:1, it is an indication that when you play the role it may often be perceived negatively by the observers. The simplest strategy to correct this is to reduce the extent to which the role is played (just do it a bit less), which usually restores the ratio to an acceptable level. In this sample report, there are many disallowable weaknesses on PL and RI.

Note: You should not try to correct or eliminate the negative portions of the bars unless they are disallowable. Tolerate them because they are linked to the strengths you see.

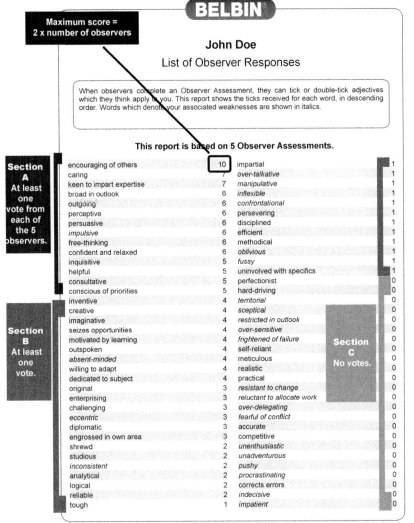

BELBIN®

John Doe
List of Observer Responses

When observers complete an Observer Assessment, they can tick or double-tick adjectives which they think apply to you. This report shows the ticks received for each word, in descending order. Words which denote your associated weaknesses are shown in italics.

This report is based on 5 Observer Assessments.

Section A At least one vote from each of the 5 observers.

encouraging of others	10
caring	7
keen to impart expertise	7
broad in outlook	6
outgoing	6
perceptive	6
persuasive	6
impulsive	6
free-thinking	6
confident and relaxed	6
inquisitive	5
helpful	5
consultative	5
conscious of priorities	5

Section B At least one vote.

inventive	4
creative	4
imaginative	4
seizes opportunities	4
motivated by learning	4
outspoken	4
absent-minded	4
willing to adapt	4
dedicated to subject	4
original	3
enterprising	3
challenging	3
eccentric	3
diplomatic	3
engrossed in own area	3
shrewd	2
studious	2
inconsistent	2
analytical	2
logical	2
reliable	2
tough	1

impartial	1
over-talkative	1
manipulative	1
inflexible	1
confrontational	1
persevering	1
disciplined	1
efficient	1
methodical	1
oblivious	1
fussy	1
uninvolved with specifics	1
perfectionist	0
hard-driving	0
territorial	0
sceptical	0
restricted in outlook	0
over-sensitive	0
frightened of failure	0
self-reliant	0
meticulous	0
realistic	0
practical	0
resistant to change	0
reluctant to allocate work	0
over-delegating	0
fearful of conflict	0
accurate	0
competitive	0
unenthusiastic	0
unadventurous	0
pushy	0
procrastinating	0
corrects errors	0
indecisive	0
impatient	0

Section C No votes.

Page 8: List of Observer Responses

How to Read This Page

This page lists the actual words checked off by the observers on their assessment forms. All of the individual observers' responses have been added together to create this summary. This page represents the detail behind the bar charts represented on page 5 of the report.

Each observer was given instructions to check any phrases which are representative of you, and to "double check" a few phrases which are very, very much typical of what they see you doing. Thus, the maximum score for any phrase on this sheet is twice the number of observers. Since this person had 5 observers, the maximum score would be 10.

Note: Phrases in italics are associated with the allowable weaknesses of a certain role.

Areas to Investigate

Break the report into three sections. Section A represents the "unanimous" attributes. The cutoff score for this section will be equal to the number of observers you had (anything with 5 or more votes in this example).

Section B consists of scores from 1 to the cutoff above. This represents attributes occasionally seen.

Section C is comprised of attributes never seen; they have scores of 0.

BELBIN®

John Doe
Team Role Feedback

This report offers guidance and advice on the best way to manage your behaviour at work and make the most of your Team Role contributions. The applicability of the advice may vary depending on the stage of your career and your current working situation.

This report is based on your Self-Perception plus 5 Observer Assessments.

You are someone who is well-placed to help develop opportunities by meeting people and finding out what is going on in other places. Within the organisation, you are likely to take a leading role in helping employees to contribute as fully as their capabilities allow to the achievement of the overall objectives. Your ability to communicate effectively is your greatest strength.

If you encounter problems, it could be because you allow enthusiasm and optimism to run away with you, without a reality check. There is a further risk that, in your desire to communicate, you are inclined to talk too much and neglect the significance of silence on the part of others which can hide unexpressed opposition. Once you realise this, there is every prospect that you will deal with the matter very effectively.

On the whole, you will be happiest working with those who interact freely and without reservation, allowing you to develop ideas. With you as a manager, any team should grow to become greater than its individual parts with each individual contributing and communicating effectively. You would work best for a manager who acts as a grounded adviser, offering a cautionary approach to new ventures and helping you towards the best decisions when you are faced with a large number of options.

Your working style should be one of facilitating innovation and progress by using all resources at your disposal – including other team members – and by using your social skills to encourage and enthuse others.

You also seem to have a propensity for taking an interest in, and caring for, others. Focus on cultivating a good atmosphere in the team by developing good relationships with others and offer to take on work which seems to have fallen through the gaps. Your efforts should earn you not only popularity but also a reputation as a considerate, diplomatic individual who can be relied upon to keep things running smoothly.

On a final note, you need to take account of the role for which you are least suited. You do not appear to have the characteristics of someone who attends to the details which can make or break a project. If you can work in harmony with someone who has these complementary qualities, your own performance is likely to benefit.

Page 9: Team Role Feedback

How to Read This Page

This page is based on the complete profile. The statements it contains have been compiled based on interviews with numerous people who have Belbin profiles similar to yours. As a result, you will likely find many items of interest to you about where you can be most successful or where you should exercise caution.

The descriptions contained in this narrative are based on the OVERALL rankings from the bottom of the first page. Specifically, it is based on the top two roles and the very last role (thus roles number 1, 2, and 9 on the last line of page 1).

Note: The descriptions on this page are directionally correct, not "gospel." The accuracy of this page typically improves once a consistent and coherent profile emerges.

*For More Information About
the Belbin Process and
Team Role Evaluations:*

BELBIN North America

www.improvingteams.com

877-333-3606

416-483-7380

www.3circlepartners.com

What is poor interaction costing you?

Effectiveness in today's workplace relies on how well people can pool their talents, resources, and knowledge to achieve results. Data from 3Circle Partners demonstrate there is a big gap between what people and groups actually achieve and what they could achieve if they could interact more effectively.

Close the Interaction Gap explores the most common causes of interaction gaps and provides practical steps for improving the effectiveness of individuals, groups, and organizations.

Learn more at 3circlepartners.com

Printed in Great Britain
by Amazon